I0021916

# Decentralized

*Blockchain and the Future Web:*

*An Introductory Guide*

# © Copyright 2018 - All rights reserved.

The content contained within this book may not be reproduced, duplicated or transmitted without direct written permission from the author or the publisher.

Under no circumstances will any blame or legal responsibility be held against the publisher, or author, for any damages, reparation, or monetary loss due to the information contained within this book. Either directly or indirectly.

Legal Notice:

This book is copyright protected. This book is only for personal use. You cannot amend, distribute, sell, use, quote or paraphrase any part, or the content within this book, without the consent of the author or publisher.

Disclaimer Notice:

Please note the information contained in this document is for educational and entertainment purposes only. All effort has been executed to present accurate, up to date, and reliable, complete information. No warranties of any kind are declared or implied. Readers acknowledge that the author is not engaging in the rendering of legal, financial, medical or professional advice. The content of this book has been derived from various sources. Please consult a licensed professional before attempting any techniques outlined in this book.

By reading this document, the reader agrees that under no circumstances are is the author responsible for any losses, direct or indirect, which are incurred as a result of the use of information contained within this document, including, but not limited to, —errors, omissions, or inaccuracies.

Table of Contents

## Contents

### *CHAPTER 1: THE EVOLUTION OF THE WEB.4*

Web 1.0 and Web 2.0.................................................5

An Introduction to Web 2.0........................................6

Web 3.0.....................................................................9

Drawbacks................................................................14

### *CHAPTER 2: THE CENTRALIZED WEB........16*

The centralized web................................................16

Challenges of a centralized web..............................18

Statistical impact of cybercrime..............................22

Statistics...................................................................22

Data Breaches..........................................................24

Single points of failure ...........................................30

Safeguards................................................................33

### *CHAPTER 3: AN OVERVIEW OF*
### *BLOCKCHAIN TECHNOLOGY ......................41*

Blockchain Technology Overview..............................41

A distributed database.............................................42

Google Docs analogy for Blockchain.........................43

A Brief Introduction to Blockchain...........................44

Accountability and the removal of trust...................47

Blocks and Hashing................................................50

Consensus.............................................................53

Proof of Work........................................................54

How it all works.....................................................55

Smart contracts.....................................................57

Salient Blockchain features..................................60

## CHAPTER 4: THE EVOLUTION OF BLOCKCHAIN...................................................62

First Generation....................................................63

Second Generation...............................................64

Current Limitations..............................................66

Third Generation..................................................68

## CHAPTER 5: KEY ASPECTS OF THE BLOCKCHAIN TECHNOLOGY.......................72

Smart Contracts....................................................72

Benefits and Limitations of Smart Contracts...............76

Smart Property.....................................................78

Oracles.................................................................80

Distributed Ledgers..............................................81

## CHAPTER 6: THE DECENTRALIZED WEB...85

Features of Web 3.0..............................................86

How Will the Decentralized Web Work?..................88

Advantages of the Decentralized Web...................90

Challenges with the Decentralized Web........................93

## CHAPTER 7: ETHEREUM AND THE DECENTRALIZED WEB ..............................94

How Does Ethereum Work.........................................94

What Can Ethereum Do? ...........................................96

Benefits of Ethereum's Decentralized Platform...........99

Examples of Ethereum Dapps....................................102

## CHAPTER 8: DECENTRALIZED APPS ........103

Benefits of Dapps......................................................104

Challenges of Dapps..................................................104

To sum it all up: .........................................................106

# CHAPTER 1: THE EVOLUTION OF THE WEB

Before the 1980's, personal computers were not a common thing, and the digital world of social media and Wi-Fi connection was far from the public's imagination. People used landlines, and even after the first mobile phone was introduced in 1973, it was far from the internet-accessing smartphone technology we now use. Letters were sent through the post office, events were recorded in diaries and most friends were made in person.

Life as we know it has been made extremely convenient through technological advancements in the World Wide Web (WWW), and more importantly, globalization has been further advanced through it. However, many people use the words internet and WWW interchangeably, when in fact they are two different things. When we refer to the internet, we are speaking of an enormous combination of billions of computers and other connected devices that are situated worldwide and linked via cables and wireless signals. This massive network is characterized by devices that comprise large mainframes, desktop computers, laptops, smartphones, personal tablets, smart home gadgets, and many other devices.

The web, however, refers to the information-sharing side of using the web i.e. you have to access the internet to view the World Wide Web or other web pages and their contents. It is the broadly used name for the HTML pages that are viewed on the internet. The web is made up of billions of digital web pages that can be viewed on your computer through web browser software. It was invented in 1989 by Sir Tim Berners-Lee, and since it was created, it has gone from a read-only web to an interactive web that promises to advance us into the age of advanced artificial intelligence. Below is a basic background on how the two work.

## Web 1.0 and Web 2.0

The first installation of the web is called the Web 1.0 and features a web that is made up of a system of interlinked, hypertext documents that are accessible through the Internet. It is characterized by the creation of read-only web pages that have very little user interaction or content contribution. The main goal for the content creators was to establish an online presence and provide information to the public. Therefore, users were only able to use the internet to read information on websites.

## An Introduction to Web 2.0

In 2004 O'Reilly Media coined the phrase Web 2.0, which refers to a proposed second generation of web-based services that include:

1. Social networking sites: Social networks connect people with all different types of interests, and one area that is expanding in the use of these networks is the corporate environment. Businesses are beginning to use social networks as a means of connecting employees and helping employees to build profiles

2. Wikis: are websites that allow visitors to easily add, remove, and edit available content, typically without the need for registration. This

ease of interaction and operation makes the wiki an effective tool for mass collaborative authoring.

3. Communication: Web communication protocols are a key element of the Web 2.0 infrastructure. Two major ones are REST and SOAP.

4 REST (Representational State Transfer) indicates a way of accessing and manipulating data on a server using the HTTP verbs GET, POST, PUT, and DELETE.

5 SOAP involves posting XML messages and re□uests to a server that may contain □uite complex, but pre-defined, instructions for it to follow. In both cases, access to the service is defined by an API. Often this API is specific to the server, but standard Web service APIs are also widely used (for example, when posting to a blog).

6 Folksonomies: Tags are personalized labels for describing Web content - web pages, blogs, news stories, photos, and the like. Collectively, the set of tags adopted by a community to

facilitate the sharing of content is known as a folksonomy.

Web 2.0 services share many attributes. But what create competitive advantage and prompt fast growth? By tracking the services that embrace Web 2.0, we can identify attributes that have made a difference.

The Foundation Attributes that enable the economics of Web 2.0, such as the network effect, the Long Tail, and user contributed values, pre-date other attributes by several years and exist in many non-Web 2.0 services. They allow services to scale efficiently to accommodate many customers. (e.g., email and bulletin boards).

The Experience Attributes create uni☐ue service experiences like decentralization, co-creation, remixabilty and emergent systems that were undeliverable before Web 2.0. Users can tailor services and systems to create new, relevant experiences that meet their needs on their terms.

Early users of the phrase "Web 2.0" employed it as a synonym for "Semantic Web," (The Semantic Web is an evolution of the World Wide Web in which information is machine processable, rather than being only human oriented), thus permitting browsers or other software agents to find, share and combine information more easily. And indeed, the two concepts complement each other. The combination of social-networking systems such as a Friend Of Friend (FOF) and XHTML Friends Network (XFN) works with the development of tag-based, delivered through bogs, and Wikis, and sets up a basis for a semantic web environment.

## Web 3.0

Although there is a clear difference between Web 1.0 and Web 2.0, the differences between Web 3.0 and Web 2.0 are not as clearly defined and often it is harder to distinguish between the two. However, there are certain characteristics between the two that can help us separate one from the other. Keeping in mind that there are various definitions and features of the Web 3.0, we will only discuss its features within the context of this book's focus, for relevance's sake.

One of the key features of the Web 3.0 is that it comprises the semantic web. The semantic web refers to the idea of turning the web from a vast collection of disconnected web pages, into a single repository of information. It also includes metadata, which can be read by other computers. Metadata is data that is about data, for example, it is a description of data. This means the semantic web makes it possible for the computer to distinguish between 2018 (a date), 2018 (a number), and 2018 (a movie name).

Sir Tim Berners-Lee came up with the idea as a means to creating a more intelligent and intuitive web. Meaning and understanding are the fundamentals, in the semantic web, for allowing the sharing of data for everyone. This means that the semantic web enables people and computers to work in cooperation, by providing users with information that has a well-defined meaning.

An example of how the semantic web can enhance the user's web experience can be illustrated by the way in which it offers an improvement to search engines. Currently, when we search the web, the search engine retrieves pages or documents that match our keywords. It is usually effective, but not 100% because sometimes we receive more results than is necessary, and some of the results do not match our search intentions. This is because the method of retrieving the document, used by the markup language (often HTML), is to simply match the results using a description of the documents. This is not always effective because, in computer language, the description is merely text that has no meaning to it. Therefore, the semantic web seeks to improve this function by providing a structure or format that can help machines understand the meaning of the web page data. Basically, what makes the semantic web different is that the search can access metadata descriptors to be able to understand what the website is about, and not just matching keywords. Thus, enabling the search to retrieve web pages based on the information contained within.

Another key feature of the Web 3.0 is in terms of connectivity and ubiquity (which means being very common or the capacity to appear everywhere). The semantic metadata function in Web 3.0 enables information to be more connected. And ubiquity in terms of Web 3.0 means that content will be accessible to multiple applications, where every device is connected to the web and the services can be used everywhere. Internet experts propose that Web 3. 0 is going to give us the experience of having a personal assistant who knows virtually everything about the user and has access to all the information on the Internet, in order to answer any question.

Let's consider this idea by looking at an example that helps to illustrate what the Web 3.0 has to offer. When you are planning a vacation, there are several factors to consider such as the location and your travel budget including flight tickets. If you decide to go to a warm and tropical destination, and you have a budget of about $2,000 for the trip, you would naturally begin your vacation planning online, in order to find the best vacation spots and deals. The whole process of comparing different budget travel websites to compare rates for flights, hotel stay, activities etc., may take several hours, if not a few days. With Web 3.0, it is believed that you can allow the internet to perform the whole task of planning your vacation, with just a simple search service. By narrowing the parameters of the search, the browser would gather the data, analyze it, and present it to you in a way that you would be able to make comparisons in a much simpler manner. Search results would include vacation spots under $2000, along wia list of fun activities and great restaurants. It would be able to better serve you in this manner because it understands the search along with the context, as opposed to just matching your keywords to web pages, which are sometimes not relevant to your search.

One of the most important elements of the semantic web is that it is not built on documents, but instead, on databases. This means that web platforms may eventually become obsolete because data will not belong to certain individuals, rather, it will be shared amongst users. In fact, many compare Web 3.0 to an enormous database, and while Web 2.0 works with the Internet to make connections between people, Web 3.0 will work to make connections with information. Experts differ on how the Web 3.0 will affect the web as we currently know it. Some think Web 3.0 will replace the current web while others think it will co-exist as a separate network.

**Drawbacks**

One of the major shortcomings of Web 2.0 is that it has evolved to become highly centralized around very large platforms that operate out of massive data centers. This creates several issues concerning control, security, privacy, and concentration of power in the hands of large organizations. It is only presently that these concerns are beginning to enter mainstream dialogue.

Web 3.0 is poised to disrupt the entire technology paradigm seeing as the critical transformation that it promises involves decentralizing the web, and only recently has this notion started to become something feasible with the development of the blockchain. Although blockchain technology is only one of many technologies that will work to achieve this, it is definitely a major advancement in the Web 3.0. In this book, you will understand why there is a need for a decentralized web, how it can be achieved, and explore the blockchain technology behind it to see why it is appropriate for the task.

## CHAPTER 2: THE CENTRALIZED WEB

In 2016, the first Decentralized Web Summit took place, where an early group of builders, policymakers, journalists, and archivists came together to "Lock the Web Open" for good. Currently, the web is in a centralized state in which it is not private, secure, reliable, or free from censorship. However, in order to fully appreciate why there is a need for a decentralized web and its importance, we need to understand the centralized web, how it functions, its benefits and its shortcomings.

### The centralized web

Originally, the plan was not for the web to be centralized, neither was it centralized in the beginning. People could add content to the web without relying on a specific service provider. Although theoretically speaking, no one entity owns all of the network or infrastructure that connects the web, and the basic protocols of the Internet and the web are not centralized, thus, the web is still decentralized in that regard. However, the emergence of, and dependence on, web service providers have created a centralized web, with the key players being large, market-dominating corporations that own all of our data.

The interactive Web 2.0 we previously discussed has given us convenient and efficient internet services that revolutionized our social interactions. It has brought together the world and has furthered globalization by bringing together producers, consumers of information, and goods and services. However, these services have been made available to us through middleman platforms. Most of these platforms provide us with their services free of charge, and for those that do not offer free services, they offer theirs at very affordable costs. For example, long distance calls which were once very expensive for many are now affordable as one can make free calls online through social media platform service that offers text, voice and video calling. Also emails, which replaced most of the post office communication route, have also made communication much more efficient for both individuals and organizations worldwide.

Moreover, employees who work for these large web service platforms are gainfully employed, with jobs that have good working environments and great remuneration packages. However, with all the convenience and good social impact that web service platforms have given us, there is now a rising concern due to the challenges that have arisen from centralized web structures.

## Challenges of a centralized web

A lot of the websites we sign up for in order to use their services, use our personal information to build our profile on their platform. They own all of our data while dictating to us how they will hold it. We often have to sign terms of the agreement in order to enjoy their services, and we do not have the option to reciprocate terms back to them, nor do a follow up on how their data controls are holding up. Instead, they dictate all rules for the transactions we partake in when using their services. This raises the important issue that lies in the hard fact that we trust these companies with all of our data, blindly.

Over the years, companies such as Facebook and Google have come to dominate the services that support the internet, and even the word Google is being used as a verb. These companies have a large share of users' attention and data, and they earn huge revenues from other companies who buy advertising space to improve their online presence and have their content discovered on their networks. Whereas people used to be in control of the news they read, by going directly to the news websites or blogs of their choice, Pew Research Center reported that social media platforms such as Facebook are dictating what news most users in the U.S they should read.

This enormous amount of power has made these companies the gatekeepers of information and we have no choice but to trust them to act fairly and responsibly when using their power. For example, if Zuckerberg were to decide that it would be in the company's best interest to give fake and misleading content to the users, thereby abusing his power, there's absolutely nothing that can stop him. Or if Google were to decide to manipulate search results to show results in favor of its own bottom line, and to the disadvantage of its competitors, there's not much anyone can do.

Fairly speaking, these companies worked hard and came up with innovative ideas and provided easy-to-use and efficient platforms for users to communicate, publish and discover content, which encouraged more users to sign up for their services. However, as they grew in size and power, they made it harder for others to compete with them and they have acquired a near-exclusive share of their respective markets. Now, these big companies are dominating the market in web service platforms, and it is very difficult, if not impossible, for start-ups to compete with these giants.

Start-ups used to have the power to push new ideas into the tech landscape and disrupt it with new innovation. In fact, Facebook, Google, and Amazon all started from that point and rose to power through this same principle, and have now become one of the five biggest and most valuable tech companies in the world. But now that they are the dominating giants in their respective markets, they make it hard to recreate their success. If anything, start-ups that attempt to follow in their footsteps are often acquired or destroyed by the competition. This only works to further reinforce the power around these powerful companies as there are no threats of competition taking them down, therefore they do not have to be concerned about users leaving for a better service elsewhere, as there is no other alternative.

Web service platforms keep all of their data in data centers. They each own the data centers where they store all of their user data, and it is where they run their applications from. The problem with these centralized structures is they are storing all of their data in one location, which leads to very serious privacy and security concerns, in that they are vulnerable to cyber attacks. In fact, Warren Buffett claims that the biggest threat to mankind, and an even bigger threat than a nuclear weapons threat, is a cyber-threat.

Every year, various companies are faced with the challenge of cybercriminals robbing their data and money, and the data volume they steal is astounding. According to Lloyds, a British insurance company, the damage of such hacks is costing businesses around $400 billion a year. The worst part of it all as reported by findings from the World Economic Forum (WEF) is that a good portion of cybercrime that takes place is undetected or unreported. Often, companies prefer not to report such events in order to prevent adverse consequences such as legal action, reputational damage, or trouble with regulators.

## Statistical impact of cybercrime

An even grimmer picture has been painted by a report from market research firm Cybersecurity Ventures called the Cybersecurity Market Report, in which it shows that every business is at risk of being hacked. It is therefore not surprising that the cybersecurity industry has experienced an exponential increase in growth.

## Statistics

Consider the following statistics in order to grasp how hackers have a major adverse impact costs to society. In 2016, cyber-security expenditure for the U.S. government was at $28 billion, and it was expected to rise in 2017 to 2018. This is a 373% increase from

2007 when the U.S. government's expenditure on cyber-security was at $7.5 billion. For perspective, consider that $7.5 billion is much greater than most budgets of many countries even in 2017. Microsoft revealed that the potential cost of cyber-crime to the global community is a staggering $500 billion, with a data breach cost amounting to $3.8 billion for the average company. According to Juniper Research, data reveals that by 2020 the average cost of a data breach will exceed $150 million, and by 2019, the cost to businesses directly linked to cybercrime will reach over $2 trillion. This is four times greater than the cost to businesses in 2015.

Also, in 2017, ransomware attacks saw a rise by 36 percent, and presently the FBI reported that attack numbers reach 4000 each day. Hackers introduce more than 100 new malware families and ransomware attackers demand on average $1077. This is an increase of 266 percent, and the amount is expected to increase in 2018. Statistics also show that 1 in 131 emails contain malware and the number is expected to increase, as hackers attempt to generate money by using malware in the same manner that they use ransomware. According to Panda Security, there are

230,000 new malware samples are created each day, and the number is predicted to rise.

Furthermore, according to a comprehensive study by Javelin Strategy & Research, identity fraud victims in 2017 were 6.5 percent of people, with the result that people were defrauded of money amounting to about $16 billion. And although major companies are the main target for hackers, 43 percent of cyber attacks have been targeted towards small businesses.

Lastly, statistics show that 90 percent of hackers conceal their track through encryption and that that businesses detect breaches on their networks every 197 days, which means it takes a company more than six months to realize that they have been compromised, and this may largely be due to the fact that hackers are becoming more sophisticated.

## Data Breaches

Centralized architectures give rise to severe privacy concerns. Users are not well informed about what goes on behind the walls of centralized services.

Therefore, they are not aware of precisely how much data these services are collecting about them, nor what they use it for.

Consider the material amount of data that has landed in the hands of malicious third parties due to a company's data breach. A good example of such an incident is the data breach at one of the largest credit bureaus, Equifax. The incident was the result of the credit reporting agency neglecting to take proper care to properly encrypt their customer's data and to patch its systems. It resulted in hackers stealing sensitive data, including personal information and the social security numbers of more than 145 million people. To make matters worse, the company only reported the incident two months later from when it occurred. The impact of the data breach could have far-reaching effects for years because the data stolen could be used for identity theft.

It is known that credit firms like Equifax sell data to third parties such as banks, employers, and landlords in order for them to learn more about the customer they are getting involved with, however, it cannot be assured just as to how secure our information is when it is entrusted with these firms.

Another similar incident worth noting occurred around mid-2015 involving Ashley Madison, an extra-marital affair dating website, which was attacked by hackers in 2015, and they saw more than 10GB of their user data leaked. Allegedly, the hackers, who call themselves the Impact Team, had two reasons behind their motive. Firstly, they did not agree with the core mission of Ashley Madison, which was to arrange affairs between married parties. And secondly, they did not agree with Ashley Madison's business practices, particularly the $19 fee that users had to pay in order to receive the privilege of having their data deleted from the website (which would later prove otherwise). The hackers published information of all of its 37 million users, after targeting and breaching the data servers of Ashley Madison's parent company, Avid Life Media (ALM).

The hackers held ALM at ransom and ordered them to permanently shut down their website or have user data published. The data was published to the open web including ALM's internal documents and usernames, addresses, phone numbers, passwords, and credit card transactions, and the leaked material began surfacing on Twitter and other such social media platforms. The CEO of ALM at the time, who later resigned, was also compromised by the data dump, which revealed sensitive personal information, as he was part of the user base on the Ashley Madison website.

Although ALM faced lawsuits against them, and although they announced a reward of 500,000 Canadian dollars for information that could lead to the hackers' arrest, there have been far-reaching consequences as a result of the data breach. Two suicides were reported to have possible ties to the incident, and scammers and extortionist have targeted users affected by the data dump, either claiming to be able to erase the leaked information, or blackmailing users to pay a price or face public shame. Furthermore, many users attempting to erase the data have downloaded malware through false websites posing as legitimate cyber-security services that offer services to clean up the data dump list.

Just recently, in early 2018, the Facebook data breach incident involving the data of most of its 2.2 billion users being mined by Cambridge Analytica, a political consulting firm, was circulating in the news. The revelation of the data breach scandal came weeks after the Cambridge Analytica scandal was exposed, which involved the improper gathering and misuse of personal data belonging to 77 million users.

Allegedly, Facebook discovered that the data had been mined in 2015, and did not alert users. Facebook CEO Mark Zuckerberg has admitted to the data breach incident, and apologized, stating that the 2.2 billion Facebook users should assume that their public profile information has been compromised by malicious third-party scrapers. He also revealed that the third parties involved took advantage of the platform's search tools over the course of several years, in order to discover user identities and to collect information on its users worldwide. Facebook has since disabled the feature that enabled malicious third parties to scrape public profile information, a feature which allowed anyone to search for users using phone numbers or email addresses.

An app called this is your digital life, built by an academic of the Cambridge University Aleksandr Kogan, and in collaboration with Cambridge Analytica, was used to collect user information. Participants in the hundreds of thousands were paid a fee to take a personality test, in which they consented to have their data collected. However, the app harvested the users' friends' data as well.

Whistleblower Christopher Wylie, of Cambridge Analytica, estimated that the amount of people compromised by the personality test is more than 50 million. He mentioned in an interview with NBC's Meet the Press, that although Facebook is starting to rectify the damage, it wasn't watertight to say that they can ensure that all the data is forever gone. He has also mentioned to the Observer that they exploited Facebook to harvest the profiles of millions of people, which they used to build models to exploit what they know about them (meaning users) and target their inner demons. He added that the company was built on that basis.

Although these examples of data breaches seem like unique cases, it is actually known that all major internet companies have some sort of history of somehow giving away user data to government agencies or selling them to third parties without the consent of their users, or just simply not taking good enough measures to protect user data.

## Single points of failure and Denial of Service (DoS) attacks

Other forms of a cyber attack that make centralized architectures vulnerable are Denial of Service (DoS) or Distributed Denial of Service attacks (DDoS). Like data breaches, the effects of these attacks are devastating to users, due to single points of failure.

Usually, a DoS attack involves the hacker sending excessive messages that request the user victim's network or server to authenticate requests which do not have a valid return address. The user's network or computer will attempt to send authentication approval, however, because it will not be able to find the return address of the attacker, the server will wait before closing the connection. Once the server is done waiting and closes the connection, the attacker sends more authentication messages with invalid return addresses. Hence, the process will start again, causing the server to wait, effectively keeping the network or server busy. The goal of a DoS attack is to cause ineffective or inaccessible services, to interrupt network traffic, and interfere with the internet connection.

On the other hand, a Distributed Denial of Service (DDoS) attack is one which involves the hackers attempting to overwhelm an online service with traffic from multiple sources, as opposed to one source such as with a DoS attack. The idea is to crash a site through enlisting a number of malware-infected devices in order to overwhelm the victim's server with illegitimate web requests. Hackers use this method to make the service unavailable and their targets can vary from a variety of important resources, such as banks or news websites, etc.

One of the major examples of a DDoS attack is the one which occurred on the 21st of October, 2016, when hackers attacked a domain name system (DNS) provider named Dyn. The attack resulted in major service websites crashing, such as Twitter, Reddit, Netflix, and Spotify, among others, as the hackers flooded the websites with illegitimate Web requests. Also, the attack resulted in a massive outage of major internet services across Europe and the U.S.

Another example of a DDoS attack involved a hacker group called Anonymous, which attacked PayPal as part of a cyber protects named "Operation Payback" and "Operation Avenge Assange". PayPal's website and services were affected for four days, because the company refused to process donation funds that were raised on behalf of the controversial programmer of WikiLeaks, Julian Assange, because of political pressure. PayPal lost thousands of dollars in business losses, and members of Anonymous were charged with misdemeanors.

These examples illustrate how centralized architectures provide cyberattackers a single target to hit. Therefore, web services such as Amazon Web Services or Google Drive can be vulnerable since they use servers to keep all of their data, and if the servers were to fail, all of the applications and websites depending on them would not function.

Moreover, the problem that these examples underline is that users do not own their own data and they surrender it to the applications and services they use. However, users are effectively locked into these services and have no choice but to stick with them or risk losing access to their data and profiles. Also, in centralized structures, the bigger the platform grows into multi-billion dollar businesses, the more insignificant the users become. They become essential only for generating data to the service provider, who in turn can do whatever is necessary to profit from it, and the users earn no share of the revenue.

One of the best ways the challenges of a centralized structure can be resolved is through the decentralization of the web. A new decentralized web can achieve an open web that allows users to control and protect their personal data better, by distributing data, processing and hosting across millions of computers worldwide, in a peer-to-peer structure, without centralized control.

## Safeguards

Like everything else, technology has got its ugly face which can no longer be ignored. With every patch released for a particular weakness, being followed by the next exploit at the very next moment, you can never be sure that your systems, your processes, your business and ultimately the economy are in safe hands. How good it would have been if technology alone could help us confide in it of totally securing ourselves? Unfortunately, that's not the case.

With a wholesome increase in internal employee frauds, gone are the days when only firewall or IDS or other security devices could protect our networks and systems. As per the 2010 Cyber Security Watch Survey, insiders were rated as the second largest threat after hackers and also the worst, since they are mostly silent and hence difficult to detect. Even a big list of policies, procedures and safe practices falls short owing to small mistakes, intentional or unintentional, by an employee. Putting money in every time does not solve the problem. You may invest millions in building thousands of security controls, but a minor inexpensive measure, if not taken, may cost you a fortune. As per the survey report, the most often neglected simple measures are listed below:

1. Patch Management: With evergrowing business re□uirements, increasing the number of software and applications fulfils them with a single constant, governing their complexity – the number of available patches. Each software vendor releases a large number of patches

continuously. The grave problem in many organizations is that the need for a patch is not realized until the business is impacted. The strategy adopted is often reactive and not proactive. The re uirement for a particular patch is at times realized six months after the patch has been released.

The other problem is unmanaged changes. Patches, if not validated, approved and tested in a disciplined manner, may cause other business functionalities or controls to break or malfunction. Challenges faced in patch management are affected by compound factors like volume and complexity of patches, the speed of implementation, impact on business, events driving the need and environment changes.

Hence, an ongoing proactive process should be followed to identify the available patches, determine the organization's need, validate, test, implement and continuously monitor the patches for compliance.

2. Log Analysis: Improper log analysis is a cause

of many unauthorized and suspicious activities going undetected. Logs are often analyzed just for complying with regulatory and legal reuirements. While focusing on compliance, an abnormal event is ignored at times. Organizations should set up rules to perform continuous analysis of daily logs to detect, alert, and act upon any suspicious activity found. While doing this, business critical assets and the activities performed on them/by them that need to be monitored, should be identified first. Also, a baseline for security configuration settings should be developed for each device/type of device within an organization and any violation to these settings needs to be alerted. All network, system and critical server logs should be closely monitored to understand the implementation and health of security controls within the organization and their compliance with organizational policies and procedures.

3. Privilege Restrictions: Unmanaged user roles and privileges are similar to open doors of a treasury which can be escalated to gain control

of critical systems within an organization. User roles and the privileges assigned to them if not managed and reviewed periodically may lead to privilege escalation attacks. Internet facing services are more risky and hence need foolproof protection against privilege escalation. There may be a few services like SSH used in the organization which re□uire complete security throughout their life cycle. All such critical services and business critical applications should be identified. A list of different users that require access to these services or applications should be prepared, and privileges should be judiciously assigned based on their roles or "Principle of Least Privilege". Such lists need to approved, authorized, and regularly reviewed.

4. Password Expiration: In spite of thousands of things said, written, talked about, and published about password security, the lack of awareness still persists. Password policies of different organizations have many aspects in common like number of characters, password history, type of characters, etc. But the

expiration period often varies in different organizations from 30 days, 45 days, 60 days or 90 days. The password expiration is always recommended to be set depending on the value of the data to be protected. Some even suggest that you never expire passwords, rather than making them weaker by users adopting unsafe practices to choose new passwords and to remember them. Too short password expiration periods might cause user inconvenience, leading to a increase in the number of help desk calls for password reset. On the other hand, too long periods have their own disadvantages of password being compromised due to user negligence or any other reasons.

There is no standard definition for password aging periods. The organization should set the expiration periods by striking a balance between data protection, password safety, and user convenience.

5. Termination of Former Employees: Off late, the cases of access controls broken by terminated employees are on a constant rise.

Disgruntled employees taking revenge by deleting all of a company's data or by hacking their own company's systems or by leaking a company's confidential information are often heard. Despite many security controls in place, improper removal of access rights of the employees who have been transferred, terminated, or resigned may lead to huge loss to business. The amount and severity of loss depends on the position, roles, and responsibilities of the employee and the privileges assigned to him/her. Organizations should follow a well-defined termination procedure with a separate checklist for removal of access rights from different systems for the IT department. Such removal should not be delayed for any reason and should be the top priority on the termination of the employee.

The list of access rights on all systems and applications should be prepared, updated, and constantly reviewed.

These minor measures if not neglected can save huge losses to an organization's business and can be of great help if implemented proactively.

However, the introduction of the blockchain technology has given us a new hope for solving the challenges faced by the centralized web. Blockchain technology has introduced the first ever decentralized currency, and since then, many other decentralized applications have emerged, bringing with them the solution to some of the major challenges of the centralized web. The following chapter will discuss this technology closer.

# CHAPTER 3: AN OVERVIEW OF BLOCKCHAIN TECHNOLOGY

## Blockchain Technology Overview

In this chapter, we will introduce blockchain technology and give an overview of the basics of blockchain technology, in order to further understand why it is trusted and preferred to decentralize the web. Blockchain was originally designed as a new kind of database, in that it is a distributed database. This means that it maintains a shared database, which is in contrast to the digital databases we've been used to, which are designed to centralize information on one computer or within one organization.

The blockchain, therefore, allows a network of computers to work together to securely record data within a shared open database, through its set of protocols and cryptographic methods. The database is made up of a series of encrypted blocks, which contain the blockchain data. It is, therefore, a continuously growing record of these blocks of data, which are linked and secured through cryptography, which makes it a trusted database. The trust is maintained by encryption and open source computer code. The blocks are linked together through hash values. In order for the database to be updated with new information, the computers connected to the database, each having a copy of the database, must come to a consensus concerning the update.

## A distributed database

Imagine an electronic spreadsheet, which is copied an umpteen number of times across a computer network. Now, imagine the computer network is designed so smartly that it regularly updates the spreadsheet on its own. This is a broad overview of Blockchain. Blockchain holds information as a shared database. Moreover, this database gets reconciled continuously.

This approach has its own benefits. It does not allow the database to be stored at any single location. The records in it possess genuine public attributes and can be verified very easily. As there's no centralised version of the records, unauthorised users have no means to manipulate with and corrupt the data. The Blockchain distributed database is simultaneously hosted by millions of computers, making the data easily accessible to almost anyone across the virtual web.

## Google Docs analogy for Blockchain

After the advent of the eMail, the conventional way of sharing documents is to send a Microsoft Word doc as attachment to a recipient or recipients. The recipients will take their sweet time to go through it before they send back the revised copy. In this approach, one needs to wait until receiving the return copy to see the changes made to the document. This happens because the sender is locked out from making corrections until the recipient is done with editing and sends the document back. Contemporary databases do not allow two owners access to the same record at the same time. This is how banks maintain balances of their clients or account-holders.

In contrast to the set practice, Google docs allow both parties to access the same document at the same time. Moreover, it also allows the viewing of a single version of the document to both of them simultaneously. Just like a shared ledger, the Google Docs also acts as a shared document. The distributed part only becomes relevant when the sharing involves multiple users. Blockchain technology is, in a way, an extension of this concept. However, it is important to point out here that the Blockchain is not meant to share documents. Rather, it is just an analogy, which will help to have a clear-cut idea about this cutting-edge technology.

## A Brief Introduction to Blockchain

### Crypto-what?

Before we get into what cryptocurrency is and how blockchain technology might change the world, let's discuss what blockchain actually is.

Simply put, a blockchain is a digital ledger of transactions, much like the ledgers we have been using for hundreds of years to record transactions such as sales and purchases. The function of this digital ledger is, in fact, pretty much identical to a traditional ledger in that it records debits and credits between people. That is the core concept behind blockchain; the difference is who holds the ledger and who verifies the transactions.

With traditional transactions, a payment from one person to another involves some kind of intermediary to facilitate the transaction. Let's say Rob wants to transfer $20 to Melanie. He can either give her cash in the form of a $20 note, or he can use some kind of banking app to transfer the money directly to her bank account. In both cases, a bank is the intermediary verifying the transaction. Rob's funds are verified when he takes the money out of a cash machine, or they are verified by the app when he makes the digital transfer. The bank decides if the transaction should go ahead. The bank also holds a record of all transactions made by Rob and is solely responsible for updating it whenever Rob pays someone or receives money into his account. In other words, the bank holds and controls the ledger, and everything flows through the bank.

That's a lot of responsibility, so it's important that Rob feels he can trust his bank otherwise he would not risk his money with them. He needs to feel confident that the bank will not defraud him, will not lose his money, will not be robbed, and will not disappear overnight. This need for trust has underpinned pretty much every major behaviour and facet of the monolithic finance industry, to the extent that even when it was discovered that banks were being irresponsible with our money during the financial crisis of 2008, the government (another intermediary) chose to bail them out rather than risk destroying the final fragments of trust by letting them collapse.

Blockchains operate differently in one key respect: they are entirely decentralized. There is no central clearing house like a bank, and there is no central ledger held by one entity. Instead, the ledger is distributed across a vast network of computers, called nodes, each of which holds a copy of the entire ledger on their respective hard drives. These nodes are connected to one another via a piece of software called a peer-to-peer (P2P) client, which synchronises data across the network of nodes and makes sure that everybody has the same version of the ledger at any given point in time.

When a new transaction is entered into a blockchain, it is first encrypted using state-of-the-art cryptographic technology. Once encrypted, the transaction is converted to something called a block, which is basically the term used for an encrypted group of new transactions. That block is then sent (or broadcast) into the network of computer nodes, where it is verified by the nodes and, once verified, passed on through the network so that the block can be added to the end of the ledger on everybody's computer, under the list of all previous blocks. This is called the chain, hence the tech is referred to as a blockchain.

Once approved and recorded into the ledger, the transaction can be completed. This is how cryptocurrencies like Bitcoin work.

## Accountability and the removal of trust

What are the advantages of this system over a banking or central clearing system? Why would Rob use Bitcoin instead of normal currency?

The answer is trust. As mentioned before, with the banking system, it is critical that Rob trusts his bank to protect his money and handle it properly. To ensure this happens, enormous regulatory systems exist to verify the actions of banks and ensure they are fit for purpose. Governments then regulate the regulators, creating a sort of tiered system of checks whose sole purpose is to help prevent mistakes and bad behaviour. In other words, organisations like the Financial Services Authority exist precisely because banks can't be trusted on their own. And banks fre□uently make mistakes and misbehave, as we have seen too many times. When you have a single source of authority, power tends to get abused or misused. The trust relationship between people and banks is awkward and precarious: we don't really trust them but we don't feel there is much alternative.

Blockchain systems, on the other hand, don't need you to trust them at all. All transactions (or blocks) in a blockchain are verified by the nodes in the network before being added to the ledger, which means there is no single point of failure and no single approval channel. If a hacker wanted to successfully tamper with the ledger on a blockchain, they would have to simultaneously hack millions of computers, which is almost impossible. A hacker would also be pretty much unable to bring a blockchain network down, as, again, they would need to be able to shut down every single computer in a network of computers distributed around the world.

The encryption process itself is also a key factor. Blockchains like the Bitcoin one use deliberately difficult processes for their verification procedure. In the case of Bitcoin, blocks are verified by nodes that perform calculations that are a deliberately prosessor and time intensive, often in the form of puzzles or complex mathematical problems, which means that verification is neither instant nor accessible. Nodes that commit the resource to verification of blocks are rewarded with a transaction fee and a bounty of newly-minted Bitcoins. This has the function of both incentivising people to become nodes (because processing blocks like this requires pretty powerful computers and a lot of electricity), whilst also handling the process of generating - or minting - units of the currency. This is referred to as mining, because it involves a considerable amount of effort (by a computer, in this case) to produce a new commodity.

It also means that the transactions are verified in the most independent way possible, even more independent than say a government-regulated organisation like the FSA, for example.

This decentralised, democratic and highly secure nature of blockchains means that they can function without the need for regulation (they are self-regulating), government or other opa☐ue intermediary. They work because people don't trust each other, rather than in spite of. Let the significance of that sink in for a while and the excitement around blockchain starts to make sense.

There are three main concepts to understand about blockchain technology, i.e. hashing and blocks, proof of work and mining, and distributed consensus.

## Blocks and Hashing

A block can be considered to be a series of blocks of data, which are securely chained to each other. Whenever users create new pieces of data, or they update existing data, they form new blocks, which are then encrypted, and assigned hash values. Hashing works in such a way that a standard algorithm runs over the block's data, and compresses it into a code (the hash) that is unique to that document. Therefore a hash value is a unique identifier of the block's content.

The data in the block is compressed into a 64-bit character secure hash, which can be recalculated from the underlying file, in order to confirm that the file's original contents have not been altered. However, given just the hash value, it is impossible to recreate the block's encrypted data content. All subsequent new blocks are securely chained to the previous block. This means that the next block's hash is dependent on the previous block's hash. Therefore, the data in any given block cannot be subsequently changed once it's been recorded, without altering all subsequent blocks.

In addition to the hash pointer linking to previous blocks, blocks contain a timestamp which shows what happened, and when it happened. Hashing and linking makes blocks inherently resistant to having their data modified, which makes them immutable, as users can write data but they cannot change it once it is in the database. Therefore, the data on a blockchain is considered incorruptible.

One method of security used in blockchain is the use of public-key cryptography. The public key is a random-looking string of numbers, which is long, and it is an address on the blockchain. When value tokens are sent across the network, they are recorded as tokens belonging to that address. There are also private keys, which are passwords that grant the owner access to their digital assets or allows the owner the means to interact with their data. Private keys and public keys work together in such a way that a user can make an encrypted transaction and send it to a public key address, however, the encrypted message will only be decrypted with the receiver's private key. This means that, in order for users to effectively ensure the security of transactions, they only have to keep the private key private, while the public key is openly distributed.

For example, when using bitcoins, in order to receive funds from another party, you use a software called a wallet, which produces a public key that you can give your counterpart, for them so send bitcoins to the address. Using your private key, you are able to access that address and access your bitcoins.

## Consensus

When blockchain is described as a distributed system, this means there is no centralized organization maintaining and verifying its database entries. Instead, the database is maintained by a large number of nodes (or computers), that are given an incentive to contribute computing resources, by earning in exchange some form of token. However, individually, these nodes cannot be trusted. Therefore, there is a requirement for the system to provide a mechanism for reaching consensus between each node, in order for them to trust the mechanism of consensus and not each other.

Any node can perform the task of validating and relaying transactions, as long as it is connected to the blockchain network using a client. The node, being a miner computer, receives a copy of the blockchain downloaded automatically when they join the network. The database automatically broadcasts new entries or changes that are made to the database across the network.

## Proof of Work

When mining nodes validate transactions, they add them to the block and broadcast the completed block to other nodes on the network. In order to deter certain service abuses, blockchain uses various time-stamping schemes, such as proof-of-work, which randomize the processing of blocks across the nodes.

Proof of work is a system that requires a substantial amount of effort by usually requiring computer processing time. It requires a challenge to be solved, and the challenge is such that no one participant on the network can solve it consistently more times than other participants on the network.

In the bitcoin blockchain, in order for miners to add the next block to the chain, they have to solve a difficult cryptographic puzzle, for which they compete to solve first, before anyone else in the network. Whoever is the first to solve the puzzle is the winner, and they are rewarded for their hard work with a small amount of newly created bitcoins, along with a small transaction fee. A consensus algorithm, such as proof of work, aims to guarantee that the next block in a blockchain is the single and only version of the truth. It helps to restrict users with bad motives from corrupting the system.

## How it all works

Blockchains work through encryption, hashing, proof of work and network consensus to create a secured, trusted, shared database. Once entered, the hashing and linking of blocks makes it near impossible change a previous block. However, this alone is not sufficient to ensure that it cannot be tampered with. Therefore, the proof of work system purposely makes it computationally that is much more difficult to modify the database, thus making it exceptionally difficult to modify all the blocks.

Proof of works also uses a distributed consensus mechanism to ensure that even if a user was able to modify the blocks, their database would not be the same as that of other users and, therefore, the rest of the network users would not accept the modification as the valid record. Therefore, for a blockchain to be tampered with successfully, a user would need all of the blocks on the chain to be altered, have the proof of work redone for each block, and take control of 51% of the network, in order to be validated by the network. If all of these factors are not met, it would not be possible for a user to alter blocks on the blockchain.

Indeed the bitcoin blockchain is a very good example of this seeing as it now secures hundreds of billions of dollars with this same method, with no reports of the network being hacked.

To sum it up, the blockchain is therefore tamper-proof technology, that enables a secure database that has automatic trust embedded in it, which is enabled by open source code and encryption. It is a shared database, with each user having their own copy of the database that is continuously updated to ensure that each user has a single source of truth.

It is transparent, meaning all users can view all the transactions and modifications entered into the database if they need to. Data quality and the resilience of the network is kept by massive database duplication across many different nodes on the network. There is no centralized "official" copy existing, and no user is "trusted" above others. Blockchain started out as a distributed ledger for bitcoin transactions, but it has become increasingly recognized and trusted to be secure enough to work as a ledger for recording and exchanging any value.

## Smart contracts

Where things get really interesting is the applications of blockchain beyond cryptocurrencies like Bitcoin. Given that one of the underlying principles of the blockchain, system is the secure, independent verification of a transaction. It's easy to imagine other ways in which this type of process can be valuable. Unsurprisingly, many such applications are already in use or development. Some of the best ones are:

**Smart contracts (Ethereum):** probably one of the most exciting blockchain developments after Bitcoin, smart contracts are blocks which contain code that must be executed in order for the contract to be fulfilled. The code can be anything, as long as a computer can execute it, but in simple terms it means that you can use blockchain technology (with its independent verification, trustless architecture and security) to create a kind of escrow system for any kind of transaction. As an example, if you're a web designer you could create a contract that verifies if a new client's website is launched or not, and then automatically release the funds to you once it is. No more chasing or invoicing. Smart contracts are also being used to prove ownership of an asset such as property or art. The potential for reducing fraud with this approach is enormous.

**Cloud storage (Storj):** cloud computing has revolutionized the web and brought about the advent of Big Data which has, in turn, kickstarted the new AI revolution. But most cloud-based systems are run on servers stored in single-location server farms, owned by a single entity (Amazon, Rackspace, Google etc). This shares the same problems as the banking system, in that the data is controlled by a single, non transparent organisation which presents the possibility of a single point of failure. Distributing data on a blockchain removes the issue of trust entirely and it also promises increased reliability due to the fact that it is so much harder to take a blockchain network down.

**Digital identification (ShoCard)**: two of the biggest issues of our time are identify theft and data protection. With vast centralized services such as Facebook holding so much data about us, and efforts by various developed-world governments to store digital information about their citizens in a central database, the potential for abuse of our personal data is terrifying. Blockchain technology offers a potential solution to this by wrapping your key data up into an encrypted block that can be verified by the blockchain network whenever you need to prove your identity. The applications of this range from the obvious replacement of passports and I.D. cards to other areas such as replacing passwords. It could be huge.

**Digital voting:** highly topical in the wake of the investigation into Russia's influence on the recent U.S. election, digital voting has long been suspected of being both unreliable and highly vulnerable to tampering. Blockchain technology offers a way of verifying that a voter's vote was successfully sent while retaining their anonymity. It promises not only to reduce fraud in elections but also to increase general voter turnout as people will be able to vote on their mobile phones.

Blockchain technology is still very much in its infancy and most applications are a long way from general use. Even Bitcoin, the most established blockchain platform, is subject to huge volatility indicative of its relative newcomer status. However, the potential for blockchain to solve some of the major problems we face today makes it an extraordinarily exciting and seductive technology to follow. I will certainly be keeping an eye out for it.

## Salient Blockchain features

Blockchain stores blocks of information across the network, that are identical. By virtue of this feature:

- The data or information cannot be controlled by any single, particular entity.

- There can't be a single failure point either.

- The data is hold in a public network, which ensures absolute transparency in the overall procedure.

- The data stored in it cannot be corrupted.

- Demand for Blockchain developers

As stated earlier, Blockchain technology has a very high application in the world of finance and banking. According to the World Bank, more than US$430 billion money transfers were sent through it in 2015. Thus, Blockchain developers have a significant demand in the market.

Blockchain eliminates the payoff of the middlemen in such monetary transactions. It was the invention of the GUI (Graphical User Interface), which facilitated the common man to access computers in the form of desktops. Similarly, the wallet application is the most common GUI for Blockchain technology. Users make use of the wallet to buy things they want using Bitcoin or any other cryptocurrency.

# CHAPTER 4: THE EVOLUTION OF BLOCKCHAIN

Now that we have covered the basic workings of the original blockchain design, we can consider how it has since evolved from the initial Bitcoin protocol to the second generation Ethereum platform. Presently the blockchain is undergoing another evolution, which some refer to as blockchain 3.0. Within this evolution, it is visible as to how the technology is transforming from its original form of essentially just a database to becoming fully-fledged globally distributed cloud computing.

These days, technology is scaling newer heights of success at an unbelievably fast pace. One of the latest triumphs in this direction is the evolution of the Blockchain technology. The new technology has greatly influenced the finance sector. In fact, it was initially developed for Bitcoin - the digital currency. But now, it finds its application in a number of other things as well.

## First Generation

The first blockchain was conceptualized in 2008 by Satoshi Nakamoto. Currently, nobody knows who Satoshi Nakamoto is, nor whether he's one individual or an organization, however, the concept and technicalities of blockchain are accessible in a detailed white paper, termed, "Bitcoin: A Peer-to-Peer Electronic Cash System." These ideas were first applied in 2009 as the core element that supported bitcoin, with blockchain functioning as the public ledger for all Bitcoin transactions.

The Bitcoin cryptocurrency was the first invention of digital currency that solved the double spending problem without the necessity of a trusted third party or central server. However, it was only later that people began to separate the concept of blockchain from that of its specific implementation as a ledger for bitcoin. It was soon realized later that the underlying technology had a more general application beyond cryptocurrencies, as it had the capacity to operate as a distributed ledger that monitors and records the exchange of any form of value. The bitcoin design has been the motivation for other applications and has played an important role as a relatively large-scale proof of concept.

## Second Generation

The second generation of blockchain emerged within a few years, and it was designed as a network upon which developers were able to build applications. This was essentially the beginning of its evolution into a distributed virtual computer, and it was made technically possible through the development of the Ethereum platform. Ethereum is a distributed computing platform that is open-source and public, and it is also blockchain-based. It features smart contract functionality, and it offers a decentralized Turing-complete virtual machine, which is able to implement computer programs through a global network of nodes. In 2013, VitalikButerin first defined Ethereum in a white paper that stated that its objective was to create decentralized applications. On July 30th, 2015, the system went live, and it has been a success that has appealed to a large community of dedicated developers, enterprises, and supporters.

The key contribution of Ethereum as the second generation of blockchains is that it has extended the capacity of the blockchain technology from primarily being a database that supports bitcoin transactions, to becoming an overall platform that operates decentralized applications and smart contracts. Both of which will be discussed more in the following chapters. By 2018 Ethereum has become the largest and most popular platform that is used for building distributed applications. Many applications have been built on it, ranging from social networks to identify systems to prediction markets, including various kinds of financial applications.

Ethereum is a major step forward and, with its introduction, it has become more evident where we are proceeding with the technology, which is leading us towards the introduction of a globally distributed computer. This will be an enormous, globally-distributed cloud computing platform, on which we will have the ability to operate any application at scale and speed. Furthermore, it assures us that it provides the security, resilience, and trustworthiness of today's blockchains.

However, the existing solutions and blockchain infustructure are inefficient and are much similar to an extremely bad computer that is not capable to do much except proofs of concepts. Reaching the next level remains an enormous challenge, which requires some original and difficult computer science, including mathematical problems and game theory. The ability to scale remains the main focus in this quest, and it is a major goal of what the third generation of blockchain technology seeks to solve.

## Current Limitations

The level of mining necessary to support the Bitcoin network currently utilizes more energy than many small nations that are about equal to the size of Denmark and costing over 1.5 billion U.S. dollars per annum in electricity. Most of this has been fueled by cheap but unclean coal energy in China where almost 60% of mining currently takes place. This high energy consumption is just simply not scalable to a mass adoption. Bitcoin and Ethereum use a combination of technical techniques and incentives that ensure the accuracy of recording ownership without a central authority.

The issue is that it is hard to preserve this balance while the number of users is also growing. Current Blockchains require global consensus on the order and end the result of all transfers. Smart contracts in Ethereum are stored publicly on every node connected to the blockchain, and there are trade-offs for storing them. The downside becomes performance issues that arise due to the reason that every node is calculating all smart contracts in real time, which leads to lower speeds. Evidently, this is a cumbersome process, especially because the total number of transactions continues to increase for about every 10-12 seconds with each new block.

The volume of transactions is likewise a pre-existing constraint. With cryptocurrency, speed is measured by transaction per second or TPS. Theoretically, the bitcoin network's maximum capacity is up to 7 TSPwhilst as of early 2018, the Ethereum blockchain can manage about 15 TPS. In order to appreciate these numbers, we can compare this to Visa's network, which is able to handle more than 24,000 TPS. Likewise, Facebook can have about 900,000 users on the webpage at any given minute, which means that it is capable of handling about 175,000 requests per second.

Another concern is cost. Currently, it costs some small amount to run the network and pay the miners for maintaining the ledger. However, this is acceptable for a limited amount of large transactions, such as sending money, and not for making small transactions like buying coffee, which can not be performed by most blockchains. This is because, in their existing form, they simply can not manage to function with very massive amounts of micro-transactions, such as would be required when allowing high volume machines to machine exchanges. It would simply prove very costly to use these sorts of economies that require many small exchanges.

## Third Generation

Due to these constraints, currently, the third generation of blockchain networks are under development, such as Definity, NEO, EOS, IOTA, and

Ethereum itself. They each use different methods to try to triumph over the current existing constraints. Since entering into the facts of how these different networks function is somewhat advanced for this book, a simple overview will instead be provided.

Lightning Network is a project that aims to increase the capacities of existing blockchains. The primary idea is the fact that small and no significant transactions need not to be stored on the main blockchain. This is referred to as an "off {chain|string}" approach because small transactions can take place from the main blockchain. It functions by creating small communities wherein transactions may occur without those being registered on the main blockchain. A payment channel is created between a group of individuals with the money being withheld on the main blockchain. Participants may then transact with one another with the use of their private keys to validate transactions.

This is somewhat similar to having a tab with a shop, in which case you just mark down what you have exchanged so that you do not need to update the main record in the bank every time you make a purchase. The record remains local before setting the funds and updating the main bank records, at some time. This only requires two transactions on the main blockchain, the first one to open the transaction channel and the second one is to close it. All the other transactions take place just within that network without having it registered on the main blockchain.

This both reduces the workload on the main blockchain and enables it to operate a large number of very fast transactions within the subnetwork. By the beginning of 2018, there was a proof-of-concept operating live on the bitcointestnet, however, the system will not be completely functional until later in the year.

Another example is IOTA. The IOTA data structure is able to achieve high transaction throughput by making validation parallel, whereas existing blockchains are sequential chains in which blocks are added in regular linear chronological order. The data structure is similar to a network as opposed to a linear chain, in which processing may take place alongside each other.

The other huge difference is that there are no specialized miners in this network, which means that every node that uses the network functions as the miner. Therefore, in the IOTA network, every node making a transaction also participates actively in forming the consensus. In other words, it is involved in mining. Therefore, there is no centralization of mining within the network, which is exactly what creates bottlenecks and uses plenty of energy. Similarly, there are no transaction fees for the process of validation, and with IOTA, since it is more user-generated; the more users that use the network the faster it becomes, which is contrary to existing systems

There are several other possible approaches but it is sufficient to say that blockchain should be understood as a developing technology whose existing implementation is similar to a large-scale proof of concept that operates on an extremely inefficient system. However, through countless experimentation and iteration, hopefully, in the years to come, it will evolve into a globally distributed computer.

# CHAPTER 5: KEY ASPECTS OF THE BLOCKCHAIN TECHNOLOGY

## Smart Contracts

A contract in the original sense is a binding agreement between two or more parties to perform a certain action, and they are written or spoken agreements that are enforceable by law. Each involved party must trust the other to fulfill their obligation. Among the key technologies of blockchain 2.0 has been the development of what are called smart contracts. A smart contract is a computer code that is stored within a blockchain and it encodes contractual agreements. The contract operates by self-executing the conditions of operation which are written directly into lines of code. The code is saved and implemented on the blockchain.

Our economies are driven by a vastly intricate set of contracts that are presently created and enforced by centralized organizations, like insurance firms and banks that are supported by the ultimate centralized authority, the nation-state system. Currently, contracts almost entirely rely upon centralized third-party organizations in order for them to be maintained and implemented. Smart contracts feature the same kind of arrangement perform an obligation, but eliminate the need for the trusted third-party between participants of the deal.

This is because a smart contract is both automatically defined and executed by the computer code itself, without discretion. Therefore blockchains and smart contract technology permits people to form their own contracts that are automatically enforceable and executable by code, because they have the ability to remove the dependence on centralized systems.

Smart contracts are distributed and self-executing across network nodes, therefore, in a sense, they are decentralized because they do not exist on a single centralized server. Which means that individuals entering into a transaction with each other do not need to trust each other, and they can confidently transact with one another without depending upon third parties to initiate and maintain the rules of the exchange. Likewise, smart contracts allow independence between participants, which means they do not need to maintain further contact after the contract is launched and operating.

One example of this concept is that of a vending machine which operates algorithmically. Upon providing the source input of money and product selection, the machine executes automatically on a rule, to create the output. The exact same instruction set will be implemented each time with every purchase. Whenever you deposit money and enter a selection, the product is released. There isn't a chance of the machine attempting not to comply with the contract, or only partly complying.

Also, another example is a situation where four different parties pool their funds to create a joint investment in which they seek to make a return interest. A smart contract can be programmed on the blockchain to allocate each amount of interest payable to the corresponding wallets of each stakeholder. A smart contract is then actually just an account on the blockchain that is managed by code rather than a user. Since it is on the blockchain it is immutable, meaning it is impossible to change the code, and therefore all parties involved in the investment can rest assured that they will automatically receive their share.

The code dictates the manner in which processing is executed and no individual is given the power to change it, nor is any organization or government able to alter, censor, or manipulate it. In this respect, it can be said that "code is a law" due to the fact that the code will execute no matter the circumstance.

Certainly, for some time now, the code has been operating as the law, for example as services moved online we have been increasingly confronted with web forms that strictly control the type of inputs that are allowed. For example, if you wish to purchase a product on some websites that are U.S. based, you will be required to have a credit card with a U.S. address, and the system will automatically enforce this by not permitting you to complete the purchase if the address field is wrong.

Another example of a smart contract can be seen in a scenario involving logistics companies. A logistics company can make use of smart contracts that execute code that dictate that, if I get cash on delivery at this location then initiate a supplier request to stock a new item because the existing item was just shipped and delivered.

## Benefits and Limitations of Smart Contracts

There are numerous benefits of smart contracts. First of all, they are automatic, which means that the time and costs associated with running and enforcing them could be eliminated. Thus making them more efficient to operate. Through this form of automation, a much higher amount of transactions can take place that otherwise could not have occurred. Therefore, it is clear that distributed ledgers and smart contracts are essential to enabling a service economy whereby ownership is displaced by providing services on an on-demand temporary basis.

Secondly, smart contracts have the potential to reduce corruption. The code leaves little room for a centralized body to modify it to their gain because it is both transparent in its workings and automatically executed.

Thirdly, smart contracts are able to reduce

dependency upon centralized organizations as individuals may be able to create their own peer-to-peer contracts, thus restricting the arbitrary power of centralized organizations.

Finally, smart contracts are also able to deliver certainty as they guarantee a quite specific predetermined set of outcomes in advance, enabling all parties to know exactly what will occur and when.

However, herein also lies a few of their limitations. The automation of the execution of a contract means that they are dependent upon formal rules with well-specified inputs, and this leaves no flexibility for a variety of eventualities should the rules need to be slightly improved due to unforeseen circumstances.

For instance, an on-demand car service that is operated through a smart contract may simply shut the user out in the event that they have not paid the fee to use the car. It may not take into account the fact that it could be a life or death emergency situation.

In the real world, there are many unforeseen incidents that can take place and sometimes rules have to be flexible and adjusted to accommodate urgent situations. This is one benefit of having real human oversight as opposed to technology because people are a lot more suitable for judging such circumstances and responding appropriately to complicated unforeseen circumstances.

Therefore the degree to which contracts can be automated is relative to the sort of environment that they are operated in, moreover, in complex situations, there will most likely be the need for some type of governing body to intervene when needed. This creates new concerning issues surrounding governance that remain yet to be figured out.

## Smart Property

A combination of smart contract with blockchain-encoded property offers us the notion of smart property. Smart property is merely property whose ownership is managed via blockchain encoded contracts. For example, a financing company can use a pre-established smart contract to automatically transfer the ownership of a car title, upon complete payment of the loan installments.

The main element of smart property is managing ownership and usage of an asset by having it documented as a digital asset on the ledger and linking it to a smart contract. In some instances, physical assets could literally be managed with the blockchain. An example of this Blockchain system is Slock. It is a door lock that is linked to a smart contract on the blockchain and it manages when and who can open the lock. This allows anyone to lease, sell or share their property without the need for a middleman.

Such innovations can allow services such as parking spaces to be sublet on an on-demand basis. Airbnb rentals could become completely automated or someone with 20 bikes in Bangladesh could lease them out. With smart contract locks, the bike can have the ability to shut itself off in the event that it has not been paid for or if it has been stolen. There can be an automatic deposit system or likewise, if the individual liked. They can merely pay a certain amount to buy the bike outright whenever the wanted.

## Oracles

Smart contracts function similar to algorithms. In order to operate smart contracts input values are needed and certain predefined conditions must be met. The smart contract's executes the programmatically predefined algorithms whenever a certain value is reached, thus automatically triggering an event on the blockchain. Thus the workings of the entire contract can only be as good as the input data.

Blockchains cannot gain access to data that is outside their network, and therefore it requires some type of trusted data feed that inputs to the system, such as what is referred to as an oracle. An oracle is a data feed that is delivered by an external service and created for use in smart contracts on the blockchain. Oracles provide external data and cause smart contracts to execute when certain predefined conditions are met. Such conditions could be any type of data such as weather temperature or the amount of items in stock etc.

In terms of smart contracts and blockchain, an oracle's function is to find and verify real-world incidents and provide the information to a blockchain. This information is then used by smart contracts.

Oracles are third-party services that are not a-part of the blockchain consensus mechanism, therefore, whether it is a news feed, site or a sensor, the source of information must be trustworthy.

However, in the near future through datafication and IoT pervasive sensing, this may be automated considering the use of advanced analytics. Using automated oracles that pull data from an array of sources and intricate analysis to find cross-correlations that provide a statistical assurance that shows, for example, a given event did or did not take place.

## Distributed Ledgers

As we have been discussing, the blockchain is similar to another layer of the internet which permits secure, trusted records and transactions to occur peer-to-peer between participants who might not otherwise trust one another. The trust lies in the technology, computer code, and mathematics instead of people and centralized organizations. In this respect, people sometimes speak about the blockchain as a "trusted machine" due to its capacity to allow a network where trust is established by design. Since the blockchain creates a trusted database it can operate as a record of value storage and exchange, and these records of value are referred to as ledgers.

Throughout history, ledgers have formed the backbone of our economies recording contractual agreements and payments that were set up for purchasing and selling of goods, or for the exchange of assets such as property. They evolved from records in stone, clay tablets, and papyrus and later paper and developed into the ledger books that support modern accounting. They allowed the formation of currencies, trade, financing and the evolution of banking. However, during the last couple of decades, these records have moved into the digital world as entire rooms of workers maintaining accounts have been replaced with digital computers. These computers have enabled our complex global economic system to thrive.

In this day and age, this record keeping system is once more being revolutionized as these ledgers are moving to a worldwide network of computer systems, and it is cryptographically secured, fast, and decentralized. This is what is referred to as a distributed ledger or distributed ledger technology (or DLT in short).

A distributed ledger can be defined as a ledger that is used to record any type of transaction or contractual agreement. It is supported by a decentralized network that spans across different people and locations while eliminating the necessity for a central authority. Cryptography is used to securely and accurately store all the information recorded on it, and it can be accessed using keys and cryptographic signatures. Any modifications or additions made to the ledger are shown and copied to every participant in just seconds or minutes. The participant at each node of the network is able to access the recordings shared across that network and they also own their own copy of it.

These networks provide a full audit trail of history information constantly available for examination, which is traceable back to the moment when a piece of information was created. Also, every participant in the network can receive simultaneous access to a standard view of the information. Distributed ledgers can be used with all forms of assets for the purposes of recording, tracking, monitoring, and transacting.

# CHAPTER 6: THE DECENTRALIZED WEB

The decentralized web, commonly referred to as Web 3.0, is an evolution of Web 2.0. A clear definition of Web 3.0 is not yet available, however, the term coined by John Markoff, of the *New York Times,* refers to a new revolution in the World Wide Web, into its third generation, and includes specific innovations and practices. Web 3.0 is still in development and, just as Web 2.0 didn't automatically extinguish Web 1.0, the move to Web 3.0 will take time and integration with existing online systems.

The main concept behind the decentralized web is the separation of decentralized apps, wallets, platforms, and other digital assets encompassing Web 3.0. Web 3.0 has been referred to as a semantic web, i.e. data driven. The data in Web 3.0 will come from the user. For instance, if you are a graphic designer and your internet searches relate to designs, you will receive more advertisements relating to design. Additionally, if you search for other things, such as computers, the web will store your common design searches and may pull up search queries that combine "design" and "computers."

The Web 3.0 revolution is already here, as the first signs are evident. The transformation of Web 2.0 to Web 3.0 is thought to have taken ten years and it will be the next fundamental change to completely reshape the Web.

What will Web 3.0 be like? Predicting the workability of Web 3.0 is somewhat of a conjecturing game, but it is believed that the decentralized web will be based on a technological breakthrough that will completely revolutionize the way we use the web through decentralization, as the idea, and the blockchain, as the means. Web 3.0 has largely been described as human-centered internet and will completely change human life. Below are some features that will enable us to better understand the decentralized web.

## Features of Web 3.0

1. Semantic Web

The semantic web is aimed at turning the web into a single repository of information, rather than just a vast collection of disconnected web pages. Tim Berners-Lee defined it as an addition of the current web in which information has a well-defined meaning, which allows computers and people to work in cooperation.

2. Artificial Intelligence

Web 3.0 will combine artificial intelligence with natural language processing. This will enable computers to understand information like humans, leading to faster and more relevant results based on search queries. Artificial intelligence will satisfy the needs of end users.

3. 3D Graphics

Three-dimensional designs such as museum guides, computer games, E-commerce, geospatial contexts, etc. will be employed in designing websites and services in Web 3.0.

4. Connectivity

In Web 3.0, information will be connected courtesy of semantic data. As a result, an end user's experience will evolve to another level of connectivity that leverages all available information.

5. Ubiquity

With Web 3.0, content will be accessible by human applications, meaning that every device connected to the web will be able to access a certain range of services anywhere. Additionally, Web 3.0 will be ever-present in our lives, at work, at home, on the road, and anywhere we go since it will be merged to our mobile devices which are, in turn, connected to our personal computers.

## How Will the Decentralized Web Work?

The decentralized web is still an emerging technology which will get better with time, just like any other technology. Web 3.0 will enable interaction with Dapps (Decentralized Apps) and other services. Internet users will still use a web browser to access the internet and this will be Web 2.0 user-friendly. In Web 3.0, the framework connecting users with digital services will be utterly different from Web 2.0.

Transactions will be manually signed and verified, to prevent platforms from obtaining unwarranted personal information without due cause. Web users will opt in, rather than trying, and often failing, to opt out. In Web 3.0, common web applications will be replaced with Dapps. The following are examples of Dapps and the applications that they could replace.

- The services of Dropbox or Google Drive could be replaced with services such as Storj, Siacoin, Filecoin, or IPFS technology could be used instead, to distribute and store files.

- Skype could be replaced by platforms such as Experty.io.

- WeChat or WhatsApp, could be replaced with Status.

- Frameworks such as Essential.one and EOS could replace software such as iOS and Android, thus providing gateways to the new web.

- Facebook could be replaced by Akasha or Steemit, while Brave browser could serve as Chrome, and Upwork could be replaced by

Ethlance.

The way in which the decentralized web functions is based on the separation of decentralized apps, wallets, platforms, and other digital assets making up Web 3.0. Therefore, when gaining access to these interfaces, one will require separate logins, seeds, and identities. For example, with Essentia, one can link these different platforms together via a single seed. Essentia provides proof of identity, as it operates as an encrypted key that can be associated with its owner. However, it does not provide more information than is required concerning an individual's identity.

## Advantages of the Decentralized Web

**Decentralized Control** – Web 3.0 will remove middlemen from the data equation. Blockchains, such as Ethereum, will provide a platform in which the issue of trust is solved through enforced rules which are unbreakable and data is fully encrypted. This means that large corporations, such as Alphabet and Apple, will have no control of user data. Additionally, no government entity will be capable of restricting sites or services, and no single individual will be able to control the identities of other users.

**Data Ownership** – End users will be able to exercise complete control of data, with the option of data encryption. Users will then be able to share information on a case-by-case and permission basis. Data ownership will limit global corporations, such as Amazon and Facebook, from storing a large volume of user information, such as contact information, incomes, interests, and even credit card details in their servers, and later selling it to advertisers and marketers for huge profits.

**Reduction in Hacks and Data Breaches** – Since data will be decentralized and distributed, to gain access to sensitive information, hackers will need to turn off the entire network, which could be virtually impossible. Additionally, state-sponsored tools, i.e. Vault7, will be rendered obsolete. Today, internet-providing companies are required to hand over user data or risk having the entire database hacked. These data intrusions can be a major security threat, such as terrorism, for example, the Coinbase case.

**Interoperability** – In the decentralized web, applications will be easily customized with device-agnostic capabilities. Device agnosticism is the capacity of a computing component to intergrate and function with various systems without the requirement of any additional special adaptations. The internet will therefore be capable of running on smartphones, TVs, automobiles, kitchen devices such as microwaves, and smart sensors. For instance, at present, most applications are OS-specific and are often operational on a single OS. Web 3.0 will eliminate this trend which adds expenses to developers tasked with issuing multiple iterations and updates of their software.

Permission-less blockchains – With the decentralized web, users will be able to seamlessly create an internet address and interact with the network. Users will not be barred on account of geography, income, or a host of other social and demographic factors. This will enable the quick and efficient transfer of wealth and other digital assets across country borders to anywhere in the world.

**Uninterrupted Services** – The decentralized web will minimize service denials through account suspensions. Also, service disruptions will be minimized since there will be no single point of failure. Data will be stored on distributed nodes, to ensure redundancy, and multiple backups, thereby preventing server failures or seizures.

## Challenges with the Decentralized Web

Although Web 3.0 entails an integrated web experience where computers will be able to understand and integrate information in a similar manner to the human mind, it will be faced with some serious challenges. The challenges mainly will concern issues of unauthorized access to data, manipulation of sensitive data, autonomous initiations of actions, and the development of harmful scripts and computer languages. Additionally, there will be challenges of data management which will certainly change the roles of information managers, knowledge managers, and journalists.

# CHAPTER 7: ETHEREUM AND THE DECENTRALIZED WEB

Ethereum is an open, decentralized platform that runs on smart contracts. In simplified terms, Ethereum is an open software platform that is based on blockchain technology. It allows developers to build and deploy decentralized applications. Smart contract apps run on a custom-built blockchain, which is typically a powerful, shared global infrastructure that can move value around. It can also represent the ownership of property without the necessity for third parties or middle men to legally verify and ensure that the set standards are followed. These apps enable developers to come up with markets storing registries of debts or transferring funds, following given instructions, without the need of middlemen.

## How Does Ethereum Work

Most people relate Ethereum to Bitcoin. However,

there is a significant difference between the two in terms of purpose and capability. Both operate on a distributed public blockchain network but Bitcoin offers one particular application of blockchain technology which enables it to carry online peer-to-peer transactions in the form of Bitcoin payments across an electronic cash system. Ethereum, on the other hand, focuses on running the programming code of any decentralized application. Instead of mining, as in the Bitcoin blockchain, the Ethereum blockchain enables miners to earn Ethers, which can be used by application developers to pay for transaction fees or services on the Ethereum network, thus fueling the whole blockchain.

Ethereum works through a system of virtual machines. When a program is used, a network connecting thousands of computers processes it. Contracts that are written in the specific language for smart contracts are compiled into "bytecode" containing features that are both readable and executable by the Ethereum Virtual Machine (EVM). Additionally, every node in the blockchain network holds a copy of transactions and the smart contract history of the network, in addition to keeping track of the current "state."

Every time a user performs an online transaction, all of the nodes on the network work in agreement to perform a requested function and agree that a change took place. In the Ethereum blockchain, a network of miners and nodes, rather than some authority such as a bank or a transaction company such as PayPal, takes responsibility for transferring the shift from state to state. The computation of EVM is through a stack-based bytecode language which can be upgraded to high-level languages, such as Solidity and Serpent, that can easily be understood by humans.

## What Can Ethereum Do?

Ethereum can enable developers to build and deploy decentralized applications. A decentralized application, commonly referred to as Dapp, is made up of codes running on a blockchain network and cannot be controlled by an individual or central entity, thereby serving a particular importance to its users. For instance, Bitcoin, which is the most common Dapp, seamlessly provides its users with a peer-to-peer electronic cash system, enabling online transactions in terms of Bitcoin payment.

Ethereum can also be used to build Decentralized Autonomous Organizations (DAOs), meaning fully decentralized organizations with no single leader. DAOs is run by a programming code, on a collection of smart contracts written on the Ethereum blockchain. The programming code is intended to replace the rules and structure of a traditional organization by eliminating the need for human oversight and centralized control. A DAO can be owned by anyone who can purchase tokens, which can be equated to equity shares and ownership. Tokens can further act as contributions which give people voting rights.

Some developers believe that an open, trustless blockchain platform such as Ethereum is the perfect and suitable solution to serve as the "backbone" to a decentralized, secure Web 3.0 that will decentralize digital identity and DNS. Therefore, Ethereum is regarded as the perfect ecosystem on which the decentralized web can be efficiently and perfectly run. This is due to the fact that the core protocol that makes up the Ethereum projects is supported by various pieces of infrastructure, code, and community. Ethereum is designed to provide freedom to developers, allowing them to build whatever they deem appropriate. This is achieved through Ethereum protocols, which can be generalized so that the core features can be combined in arbitrary ways. Moreover, Dapps on Ethereum, leverages the Ethereum blockchain to develop solutions which depend on on a decentralized consensus. They provide new products and services which would otherwise not be possible.

The importance of Ethereum to the decentralized web is already being seen through high-profile Dapp running on Ethereum such as Digix, Augur, and Maker which use open-source components. While each of the teams developing these Dapp is a separate organization from the Ethereum Foundation and has its own goals, all teams are undeniably benefiting from the overall Ethereum ecosystem.

## Benefits of Ethereum's Decentralized Platform

**Immutability** – The data is encrypted, preventing the third party from accessing or making changes to sensitive data.

**Tamper proof apps** – These are based on a network that is formed around the principles of consensus, thus making censorship impossible.

**Secure** – There is no central point of failure as the platform is secured using cryptographic applications which are well protected against hacking attacks and fraudulent activities.

**Zero downtime** – With the decentralization of platforms, apps will never go down and can never be switched off.

The generic definition of decentralized applications, commonly referred to as Dapp, is under intense debate and development. However, typical definitions include:

- An open-source code which is autonomously managed

- Records and data stored using blockchain, providing trustless interaction and avoiding any single point of failure

- The use of cryptographic tokens to reward users by providing computer processing power

- The generation of tokens through a cryptographic algorithm

In today's web, there are millions of applications used which follow a centralized server-client model. The centralized system is widespread and controls the operation of the individual units and flow of information from a single center in a particular app. In centralized apps such as Facebook, Amazon, and Google, to mention just a few, users are overwhelming dependent on the central power to send and receive information. These apps use stacks to provide valuable services and are usually prone to massive flaws.

Unlike centralized systems, the decentralized application system is spread across multiple nodes, rather than a single node. Each node works separately to perform a specific function. In order for an application to be considered a Dapp, it must have the following features:

**Applications have to be completely open source** – Dapps must operate autonomously and no entity should control the majority of tokens. The application may adopt certain protocols in response to feedback on proposed improvements from the market, in accordance with its users.

**The data of the application and records of operation must be cryptographically stored** – The applications' records and data have to be stored cryptographically in a public, decentralized blockchain in order to avoid incidents of central points of failures from occuring.

**Cryptographic token** – The application should use a cryptographic token, which is necessary for access to the application. Moreover, the contribution of value that miners give should be rewarded with the application's tokens.

**The application must generate tokens** – Tokens must be generated by an application in accordance with a standard cryptographic algorithm, and they act as a proof of the value that the nodes contribute to the application. For example, Bitcoin uses a Proof of Work algorithm.

# Examples of Ethereum Dapps

- Token systems

- Financial derivates and Stable-value currencies

- Identify and reputation systems

- Decentralized file storage

- Decentralized autonomous organizations (DAOs)

# CHAPTER 8: DECENTRALIZED APPS

Dapps are economizing digital resources, thereby providing ways to monetize applications which, previously, was hard to do in terms of digital assets and content. A decentralized application can also provide competitive pressure against other applications filled with too many irregularities such as malware attacks, fraud and intermediaries. This competition changes the pricing of digital resources providing its users a greater value for their money and serves a wide market of users.

Dapps can serve as a mechanism for token distribution through development, fundraising, and mining. The multiple distributions of token offer more flexibility and opportunity as compared to a centralized system, which can essentially be controlled by one main institution.

Dapps offer completely new ways and processes to conduct transactions. For example, Dapps can enable embeddable records, such as smart contracts, and they can aid with fraud prevention through the use of tokens. Also, they offer the advancement of the function of money, such as Ethereum, through distributed autonomous corporations (DACs).

## Benefits of Dapps

The key advantage of the decentralized applications is that the essential components are distributed. This improves tolerance to faults and makes it practically impossible—and expensive—to attack such a network. The backbone of Dapps-blockchain ensures fast, reliable, and secure applications which enhance the customer experience. Dapps, coupled with blockchain, provide a fast, efficient, and affordable way of processing and storing big data. Moreover, decentralization acts as a barrier to collusion, which is a factor that has often allowed corporations and government to exploit others.

## Challenges of Dapps

Decentralized applications certainly face some challenges, such as:

- Fixing bugs or updating applications will be difficult since every peer in the network will have to update their node software.

- Some applications that require the verification of user identity give rise to the challenge that is caused by the fact that there is no function of a central authority to verify user identity. Thus, this becomes a major issue while developing such applications.

- Dapp are challenging to build because they use very complex protocols to achieve consensus, also they have to be built to scale from the start itself. Therefore, it is not possible to just implement an idea and then, later on, add more features and scale it.

Additionally, ads cannot be integrated into Dapp since users are not able to check advertising standards. Clients may not display ads because there is no benefit for them in doing so.

## To sum it all up:

A decentralized web offers us to use internet services such as social networking, communication, banking etc. through user powered technology which is by the people, and for the people. This means that instead of trusting a centralized company users will have an internet that becomes a "true democracy". In such a structure, information operates on servers across client side apps or on multiple federated servers, where responsibility of services is shared by users in a peer-to-peer (P2P) distributed network via the blockchain. Users own and control how their information is shared and used, and the user can decide who to release it to and when they want to release it. Although it is still in its infancy, it offers us a promising future to the many problems of centralized web structures that have proven to have far reaching consequences.

www.ingramcontent.com/pod-product-compliance
Lightning Source LLC
Chambersburg PA
CBHW070844070326
40690CB00009B/1687